FASHIONS OF A
DECADE
THE
1960s

Yvonne Connikie

Series Editors: Valerie Cumming and
Elane Feldman
Original Illustrations by Robert Price

B. T. Batsford · London

Contents

ISBN 0 7134 6437 2

Text design by Gail Hurstfield
Jacket design by David Stanley
Composition by Latimer Trend & Co Ltd
Manufactured by Bookbuilders Ltd
Printed in Hong Kong

For the publishers
B. T. Batsford Ltd
4 Fitzhardinge Street
London W1H 0AH

THE 60S

The 1960s were a great time to be young. Youth culture and youth fashions, which had begun to take shape in the fifties, blossomed as never before. Young people in the West were benefitting from the postwar industrial boom, and had begun to refashion themselves accordingly. The existing fashion business wasn't always able or willing to deal with this shift in demand, so the youth market would largely belong to a new generation of designers. Fashion became split along lines of age.

Extra cash in young people's pockets meant extra freedom – freedom for the imagination, freedom for creative and provocative ideas. The world was becoming a smaller place, as people talked of the global village and began to believe what they were saying. The new freedom of youth made itself felt on both sides of the Atlantic, and it also began to make ripples farther afield – in Japan, Africa and Eastern Europe.

Pop makes the running

Pop music went through enormous changes too: it even began to be taken seriously as an art form. The charts were virtually taken over by young – even teenage – artists, who were making the music young listeners most wanted to hear. Biggest of all were the Beatles, four young men from Liverpool who began playing to packed nightclubs in Merseyside and Hamburg before moving on to the world stage in 1963 with an unbroken string of hit records. The Beatles' clothes and hairstyles became the most familiar symbols of the new youth culture.

Although the Beatles were the most popular group they were strongly challenged as spokesmen for youth by two other figures – singer/songwriter Bob Dylan, and Mick Jagger, lead singer for the Rolling Stones. Both Dylan and the Stones opted for a rebellious look, with outfits recalling the dress of outlaws in Western or gangster movies (and, in fact, both Dylan and Jagger have acted in such films). They gave form to Yves St Laurent's remark that "clothes were a form of protest", and both acquired a host of imitators.

In the mid sixties a black-owned record company, Motown, began to take a dominant share of the singles charts. Motown launched the careers of such megastars as Diana Ross, Smokey Robinson, Michael Jackson and Stevie Wonder. In place of a rebellious stance, Motown promoted a smart, stylish and upwardly mobile image for its artists, insisting on extensive grooming and styling before their public appearances got underway. The alliance of fashion with pop music has never been closer.

Mick Jagger in the mid sixties – cool but rebellious. Long but carefully-styled hair, casual but sharp jacket and t-shirt.

All these artists created their own distinctive styles of dress. Dylan developed from beatnik to hippie to suede-jacketed country-rocker. The Beatles moved from chic Pierre Cardin suits to the spaced-out military uniforms of the *Sergeant Pepper* period. The Rolling Stones posed as threatening, deliberately unkempt delinquents. Motown girl groups such as the Supremes dressed themselves up in gloves and satins and feather boas; male groups such as the Temptations and Four Tops went for colour-coordinated suits. The look of all these artists said something about their music and attitudes that could be understood at a glance. And the freedom that fashion allowed in the sixties meant that everyone could dress up. Everyone, in fact, could think of themselves as a performer and "do their own thing".

Twiggy's boyish looks and stick-thin figure made her the number-one model for the mini-skirt.

Couture, 1960. Dior's yellow-and-black print suit teamed with black straw hat, black "stilettoes" (high-heeled shoes), black beads and gauntlet gloves. The formality of the model's pose matches the restrained elegance of the setting.

Out of the Fifties

But the sixties had begun in a very different mood. The year 1960 seemed not so different from 1959, and the atmosphere of the late fifties lingered on until the explosion of new energy around 1963. To understand this period, we need to look at what had gone before.

Fifties fashion had been dominated by two strands that completely failed to connect – the styles of the great *haute couture* fashion houses and the sudden emergence of the teenager and teenage fashions. The fifties were in many ways also the heyday of the great Paris houses, like Dior, Givenchy, Lanvin and Balenciaga. They continued to dictate new styles of fashion season by season. Tailoring and finishing were carried out to the very highest standards, as was the case with their fashion rivals in New York, London and Milan. A more

youthful approach was beginning to take shape through the young French designer Yves St Laurent, who began designing under his own label in 1962. Though St Laurent's ideas might have been radical and new, he was seen at first as simply the latest in a long line of Paris masters of cut and style. And high fashion remained in the fifties largely the preserve of the wealthy, with relatively little impact on the dress of the average office worker, whether male or female.

Bare feet, Sloppy-Joe sweater, tight pants, outrageous behaviour – it could only spell beatnik in 1960.

Rock Stars

Rock stars gained an importance in the 1960s that went well beyond the audience for their music. Performers such as Bob Dylan, Mick Jagger, Janis Joplin and Jimi Hendrix were seen as speaking on behalf of the younger generation – both by young people themselves and by the media, who sought out their views on any and every issue. Often the stars themselves were annoyed by the pressures they felt were being placed upon them – "I'm not the leader of no organization" commented an angry Dylan. Jagger and Hendrix, amongst others, spent time behind bars on drug charges – and both were considered to have received harsher treatment from the courts because, as figures in the public eye, they were thought to be worth making an example of.

Poles apart from all this were the youth cults that sprang up: in the UK, the greasers, rockers and Teddy boys; in the USA the teenage styles reflected in the hit movie *West Side Story*. These cults were considered dangerous breeding grounds for juvenile delinquency. Standing apart from this were the beatniks, who jumped to prominence in the late fifties, particularly in California and New York. The beat culture was primarily a movement of writers, with Jack Kerouac, Allen Ginsberg and Lawrence Ferlinghetti being some of leading lights. Certain styles of dress (and a leaning toward hard-bop jazz) were a fixed part of the beatnik attitude: handmade sandals, black turtleneck sweaters, black berets and tight black pants. The beatniks' "outsider" or bohemian attitudes, mixing up popular culture with "high art", were a foretaste of what the sixties were to offer. The beatniks themselves spilled over into the new decade: in fact, the beatnik attitude has never really gone away.

Science and Technology

The "affluent society" of the West meant that more and more technological gadgets became commonplace in the home during the sixties: colour television, hi-fi record players, better cars and more sophisticated washing machines. Cheaper jet air travel led to an enormous boom in tourism. Giant strides were being made in computer technology – bringing the first desktop computers within sight – and also in medicine, with the first heart transplant operations being performed. Scientific progress seemed to be unstoppable – and anything seemed possible in the years ahead.

John Young and Virgil Grissom prepare for the launch of the Gemini 3 spacecraft, March 1965.

Space Race

In the early sixties, the Soviet Union seemed to be well ahead of the United States in the race to space. In 1961, Russian cosmonaut Yuri Gagarin achieved one complete earth orbit in the spacecraft *Vostok 1*. President Kennedy declared publicly that the US would catch up and, in 1962, John Glenn became the first US astronaut to orbit the earth, as part of the Mercury space programme. The US followed up the Mercury flights with the two-man Gemini spacecraft, and finally the three-man Apollo project. Apollo 8's flight during Christmas 1968 placed men for the first time in orbit around the moon — by far the most spectacular spaceflight to date. This feat was surpassed in July 1969 when Apollo 11 landed two of its crew on the surface of the moon — thus achieving Kennedy's pledge of a manned moon landing before the end of the decade. The Soviet space programme seemed in contrast to have lost its way after its early successes, which included the first "spacewalk" by Aleksei Leonov in 1965.

How they did it in the movies (1). Programme for the Stanley Kubrick and Arthur C. Clarke film *2001: A Space Odyssey*.

11

Mod cult

The new decade had begun to show its true face by 1963. This was the year of worldwide Beatlemania, and it was also the year that the mod cult erupted in Britain. Short for "moderns", the mods personified what the early years of the Swinging Sixties were held to be all about: youth, mobility (mods lived by their scooters), fashion (mods spared no expense on their clothes), and an intense interest in the latest sounds on the soul and R&B scene, such as Booker T and Wilson Pickett.

By 1964 the mods had acquired a bad name, following a series of pitched battles at seaside resorts between groups of mods and rival rockers – more traditional "greaser" motorcycle gangs. Mods and rockers seemed to spell nothing but trouble and by the mid sixties they had begun to fade out.

Barbara Parkins (the girl from U.N.C.L.E.) teams knee-length leather boots with a maxi-length leather coat for this 1966 publicity shot from her spinoff to the popular *"Man from U.N.C.L.E."* TV series.

Mods, 1964. Cycles, sharp suits, narrow ties and "parka" anoraks team up for a day trip to Brighton.

Quant cult

What didn't fade away was the mod enthusiasm for young, stylish fashions. The boy on the motor-scooter was replaced by the girl in her mini-skirt – a fashion breakthrough that was to remain important until the end of the decade. The term "youth-quake" was widely heard. Mary Quant was one of the first designers to take advantage of this rapidly changing atmosphere.

Quant had been designing and manu-facturing her own clothes since the late fifties. In the atmosphere of the early sixties, the young, fun fashions she designed began to take off. Her high point was undoubtedly the launch of the mini-skirt – a fashionable skirt that went eight or nine inches above the knee and stayed there, at least until the arrival of maxi and midi lengths in 1969–70. Like St Laurent, Quant moved away from the expected role of the fashion designer, produc-ing her own range of tights with origi-nal lace effects and open mesh de-signs, and starting her own range of cosmetics as well. Tights (in place of stockings) and the softer, unboned bra were essential with the mini-skirt, and pointed the way forward for women's underwear.

Mary Quant was also closely involved in the revolution that was taking place in shopping habits. From the mid six-ties on, Europe and North America began to fill up with boutiques – small clothing shops aimed at the teenage customer, and depending on a rapid turnover of stock. Mary Quant's *Bazaar* chain in the UK, which had been in business since the late fifties, was described by Quant herself as "a kind of permanently running cocktail party". Shopping for clothes became fun. Yves St Laurent was on the same wavelength, and he opened his bouti-que chain *Rive Gauche* in 1966: it quickly expanded to 160 branches worldwide. Others followed suit.

Young fashions from Yves St
Laurent's *Rive Gauche* chain of
boutiques, 1967.

Changing Times for Women?

The postwar era of the late forties and fifties had seen most women in the West still tied, or returning after war-work, to the roles of wife and mother – though the new availability of domestic gadgets did make these roles less physically demanding than before. But the turbulent social atmosphere of the sixties led to a belief that anything was possible – even a complete revolution in the relationships between men and women. Easily available and reliable contraception began to give women far greater control over their personal relationships, though by the end of the decade women had made only modest progress in terms of representation in politics, business or the professions. Indeed, many of the fashions and values of the sixties tended to push young women into a vulnerable or passive, "dolly-bird" role. A pretty girl in a mini-skirt wasn't expected to say anything intelligent.

Beach Boys (and Girls too)

The Swinging Sixties/space-age mood caught on fast in the USA. Betsey Johnson attracted attention with her gangster-stripe pants suits and clear PVC dress with paste-on-yourself stars, while Rudi Gernreich covered all bases by producing the world's first topless swimsuit and then teaming a strappy bathing costume

with thigh-high boots and a space-visor. Few actually went topless, but swimwear and the bikini in particular became briefer than ever. Established designers Geoffrey Beene and Anne Fogarty also used the mini-skirt to their advantage, Beene teaming up short skirts with long jackets and Fogarty introducing her "mini culottes".

Mods were never much of a cult in the United States, where American youth had been enjoying the cult of the automobile since the fifties, and the early sixties music of the Beach Boys and others tended to put cars first and girls second – as one can hear in the Beach Boys' song "Little Deuce Coupe". Surf music favoured a style of easy casual dressing suitable for the California sunshine, with short sleeves, and open-neck striped shirts being favourite attire for the Beach Boys themselves, together with carefully waved hairstyling. The flavour of this period is well captured in the 1973 film *American Graffiti*, with its period costumes and soundtrack. Moreover, the movie concerns one particular teenager's need to leave behind this comfortable small-town life for the larger world outside.

A hippie wedding. Notice the great variety of styles: ethnic, historic, mini, psychedelic, and even beatnik.

Violent Societies

Despite all the talk of peace and love, the world of the sixties seemed to be as violent as ever. Full-scale wars raged in Southeast Asia, in the Middle East, and in the Indian subcontinent. Russian tanks entered Czechoslovakia to crush Prime Minister Dubcek's liberalizing government. British troops were on the streets of Northern Ireland from August 1969. Riots flared up in Los Angeles, Chicago, Paris and Berlin. Others pointed to increasing crime and lawlessness: Richard Nixon found the law-and-order ticket a useful path to the White House. Assassinations also made the headlines: the most prominent public figures to be gunned down were John F. Kennedy, Robert Kennedy and Dr Martin Luther King. Street crime began to be discussed as a serious problem in some of the world's major cities. The future might have arrived, but it didn't seem to be a peaceful one.

Mary Quant in action.

Peace and War

For many small-town American youths, the bigger world outside found them in the shape of the draft and a year of duty in Vietnam. The average age of the American soldiers killed in Vietnam was just 19 years – a statistic that helps explain the increasingly political nature of American youth culture from the mid sixties on. Musicians such as folk singers Joan Baez and Barry McGuire publicly spoke out against the war, and warned of even worse catastrophe should anything like the US-Soviet confrontation of the Cuba Crisis be repeated in Southeast Asia. Many students took part in demonstrations against the war and the draft, while other Americans were horrified by the live images of fighting brought right into their homes for the first time on television. By the end of the decade, US forces were beginning to pull out of Vietnam.

Culottes, spring 1967, from the Relang collection. Much favoured by designers at this time, culottes never rivalled the popularity of the mini-skirt.

Cold War?

The Cold War between the US and USSR nearly became "hot" in 1962, when presidents Kennedy and Khrushchev clashed over the placement of Soviet nuclear missiles in Cuba, just 90 miles off the Florida coastline. With the two countries sliding towards the brink of war, Khrushchev backed down and agreed to remove the missiles. The Cuba Crisis also meant the end of Khrushchev's political career. A new, more cautious regime in Moscow, headed by Prime Minister Alexsei Kosygin and Party Chairman Leonid Brezhnev, seemed content to watch and wait, as the US entangled itself ever more deeply in the Vietnam War, while both superpowers watched the unfolding of China's Cultural Revolution with alarm. A new and unpredictable superpower suited neither of them. And while neither the US nor USSR wanted war with each other, both continued to stockpile ever more powerful nuclear weapons throughout the decade.

Vietnam

Fighting in Vietnam — then known as "French Indo-China" — in the fifties had involved French troops and the Vietcong Nationalist forces. A ceasefire had divided the country in two. The US became drawn into the renewed fighting in the early sixties on the side of the non-communist south, with President Kennedy making the initial decision to send in troops. By the mid sixties the US found itself heavily committed to a costly war that was unpopular at home and abroad: Kennedy's successor, Lyndon Johnson, lost so much support because of his commitment to the war that he elected not to run for office a second time in 1968. The Vietnam War was the cause of sharp divisions and unrest in US society, and it provided a strong political focus to many young people. The war was a particularly bitter experience for many blacks, and black leaders such as Eldridge Cleaver and Huey Newton could point to the contradiction of black Americans being sent to defend democracy in Southeast Asia while their battle for civil rights was not yet won at home.

Vietnam, 1969. Teenage GIs in combat.

Muhammad Ali – world heavyweight boxing champion and perhaps the sixties' most famous Black Muslim.

Ali refused the Vietnam draft, and was later stripped of his world title.

21

Hippie power

The hippie ideals of peace and love have often been ridiculed in the years since the sixties. It is worth remembering that the movement grew up against a backdrop of compulsory military service – at least, this was the case in the USA, where the hippie movement had its roots. Hippiedom was worldwide, and all you needed to do was to let your hair grow to join. Although at bottom a political and moral movement, rejecting Western materialism and its money-grubbing "rat race", hippies set the tone for much of the fashion of the late sixties. They set the seal on the "anything goes" attitude, mixing up ethnic and psychedelic influences, which had been building up in force for some time. In fact, the hippies had such a widespread impact that, by the early seventies, long hair and ethnic wear had become just another way of dressing up, with little or no political significance attached.

Hippie dress fitted in with the new "peacock" attitude that was affecting male dress, which was seen as suitable for a society moving toward a greater equality between the sexes. Men either dressed up as a form of self-expression or to attract women, as women had always dressed up to attract men. The declining infant mortality rate meant that, for the first time in history, there were more men than women to go round. Men needed to compete with one another to gain attention. Women were taking advantage of the chance to dress more simply – in practical trouser suits, and especially jeans. "You can't tell the boys from the girls these days" was a frequent complaint. "Unisex" dressing was the style. Young hippie men and women wore long hair, headbands, worn-out jeans and sloppy, casual outfits.

Unspecified "ethnic" and space-age influences combine in this 1967 Vancetti trouser suit. Note the textured fabric and the wildly experimental hairstyling.

A shrinking world

Another by-product of the hippie culture was the much wider acceptance of varied styles of ''ethnic'' dress, though the prime movement in this area came from Black Power organizations and black musicians. Black pop stars in particular began to drop the carefully-groomed Caucasian-like appearance and allow themselves to project a much stronger black image: Sly and the Family Stone and Isaac Hayes are good examples. Established artists such as Martha and the Vandellas began to alter their image. The black ''ethnic'' look began to be widely popular, with ''afro'' hairstyles spreading as far afield as Japan. Hardcore soul artists such as James Brown began to attract a mainstream following.

Sly and the Family Stone's afro hairstyles were as startling as the unprecedented funkiness of their music, which pointed the way forward to the dance music of the seventies and eighties.

The "ethnic" mood was also fueled by cheaper and more ambitious travel, with places as exotic as Bali or Nepal suddenly becoming realistic destinations. Much of this ethnic dressing was done for nothing more than instant effect, but the focus of fashion was beginning to extend beyond Europe and North America. The world might have been getting smaller, but the fashion map was becoming more diverse all the time.

Nevertheless, as the decade ended, it became noticeable that things had not changed as completely in fashion as many had believed. Landmarks had gone – including Balenciaga, last of the great "pure" *couturiers*, who retired in 1968. But many of the old guard fashion elite were still around. Paris might have been eclipsed in the sixties, but the city was set to make a big comeback in the seventies and eighties. Not that the French had taken a back seat in the sixties, with Courrèges and Cardin cashing in on the space-age and Op Art fever, and being only half a step behind the London designers in promoting the mini-skirt. The Apollo 11 moon landing in 1969 gave a timely end-of-decade boost to all things space-age.

Civil Rights and Black Power

The early sixties saw the growth of the civil rights movement, under the leadership of Dr Martin Luther King, climaxing in a 200,000-strong march to Washington, DC. President Kennedy's Civil Rights Bill was passed under his successor, Lyndon Johnson, but black frustrations over poor living conditions and job opportunities continued through the decade, reaching a peak during the devastating Watts riots of 1965 in Los Angeles. The Black Power movement grew up alongside this unrest. Huey Newton achieved prominence as a leader of the Black Panthers – an organization whose aim was to protect blacks from police harassment while staying within the law. Starting on the West Coast, the movement spread to several other states. A different stance was taken by the late Black Muslim leader Malcolm X, who aimed to steer black youths away from conflict with the law through religious values and a strong sense of pride in the black heritage.

Black Power demonstration at the Olympic Games in 1968.

Cult movie. Faye Dunaway and Warren Beatty in a publicity still from *Bonnie and Clyde* **(1967) – a gangster movie set in the twenties that pointed the way toward much of the retro cinema (and fashion) of the seventies.**

American, French and Italian designers were at the forefront of those seeking to transform street fashions into designer collections; Pucci, Vancetti and St Laurent were important in this area. Bonnie Cashin's work had used ethnic garments such as the poncho as early as the late fifties. Betsey Johnson, with her cowhide mini-skirt dresses, also took up this approach. The Italian designer Fiorucci began to establish his own personal niche halfway between boutique fashion and the designer label. And of course, many big names such as Chanel continued their established course, almost as if the Swinging Sixties had never happened.

The end of the sixties saw the first signs of a new conservatism, both in fashion and society. Richard Nixon was elected US president in 1968, promising to speak on behalf of the "silent majority". France turned away from radical politics after the student uprisings of 1968, while Britain elected a new Conservative government in 1970. And just as the 1960s had seen fashion reach forward into the future, rushing to embrace new or exotic ideas, the seventies were soon to be gripped by a very different mood: a nostalgic yearning for the past.

Woodstock

It began as the 1969 Woodstock Free Festival of Art and Music, and it ended as the biggest event of its kind the world had ever seen, with crowds estimated at half a million. A movie and two double albums attempted to package the atmosphere of an event in which Jimi Hendrix, Sly and the Family Stone, The Who, Santana, Janis Joplin and others performed. The event became bigger than the music, and turned into a symbol for everything connected with hippies, flower-children and the "love generation". An attempt to repeat the success of Woodstock on the West Coast at Altamont later in 1969 ended in disaster when a spectator tried to fire a shot at Mick Jagger while the Rolling Stones were performing on stage. The man was killed by members of the Hell's Angels motorcycle gang which the Stones had hired to act as a security force.

Woodstock 1969: the highpoint of the hippie movement.

Cocktails and Beehives

We'll Always Have Paris

John F. Kennedy became US president in January 1960, and his fashionable and glamorous wife Jackie became the new first lady. Much younger than their predecessors, many saw them as signs of a new hope and optimism for the new decade.

Jackie Kennedy became a prominent "model" and style-setter for the latest French fashions. Yves St Laurent (born 1936) opened his own fashion house in 1962, and quickly enhanced his reputation as the most innovative and brilliant of the younger designers. Coco Chanel — 50 years into her career — maintained her reputation for shunning all extremes, though she did, however, promote a shorter-length lacy cocktail dress, and went along with the new leaner, narrower cuts.

Still going strong from the fifties was the "bouffant" look, with skirts kept firmly in shape by underlayers of stiff petticoats. This style was developed into the "suspense jupe", with the ballooning fullness of the skirt constricted at the knee.

For some years, it had been fashionable to have the hair pulled back off the face. Suddenly, hair came alive with back-combing (teasing) and the arrival of the "beehive" style — a fuller shape, kept in place with plenty of hairspray. Women enjoyed the new freedom — wearing their hair loose, or

The 1960 cocktail dress, Italian style. Note the formality of the model, the setting, the spectators alongside the catwalk.

piling it on top of their head in a bun. And women with short hair could buy hairpieces to achieve the same effect. Even Jackie Kennedy went in for the beehive look. On a state visit to France in 1961, she seemed to make an almost bigger impact than her husband.

Move Over, Darling

Men's styles at this time were strongly influenced by Italian designers. Formality was still the keynote, even for leisure wear. Suits were single-breasted, featuring short jackets tailored with narrow lapels, worn over narrow-collared shirts and slender ties. Pants were narrower – for the young and fashionable, extremely so – with the tapering effect finished off with pointed "winkle picker" shoes. Longer hair for men was beginning to replace the crewcut short back and sides – but still firmly slicked back with oil and gel. Facial hair became more acceptable. Many men of all ages grew lavish moustaches and beards, and many let their sideboards grow fuller and longer.

Many teenage girls – especially in Europe – were still wearing clothes almost identical to their mothers. The big revolution in teenage fashion still lay in the future. Many copied the look projected by Hollywood star Doris Day – a pretty and feminine image that appealed to women of all ages. Doris Day combined a girl-next-door appearance with a glamorous and stylish film-star image, and became the biggest box office draw of the period in movies such as *The Thrill of it All* and *Move over, Darling*. The music and style of these films has often been used to recreate the atmosphere of the early sixties.

Let's Twist Again!

Elsewhere, music still rocked and rolled, and couples jived and danced the latest dance steps like the Mashed Potato. You needed to know the right steps, which were all mapped out in magazines, all ready to be copied on Saturday night. The Twist became a new dance craze. And if couples weren't twisting to Chubby Checker's famous record, they might well be necking to the ballads of Gene Pitney, Helen Schapiro, or even former rocker Elvis Presley, who returned from service in the US Army with a new clean-cut image and romantic songs such as "It's Now or Never" – a reworking of the Italian ballad "O Sole Mio".

The sixties looked set to continue very much in the vein of the previous decade: new faces, new fashions – but little change in the underlying mood or attitude. But no-one writing in say, 1960, could have been expected to foresee the enormous changes and reversals that lay in the years ahead.

29

Sharp suit. Custom-made tailoring for men remained a strong tradition, but styling went through rapid change. This 1964 suit by Hector Powe would look well on sixties fictional heroes such as James Bond or Napoleon Solo. Details include the draped shoulders, wide lapels, plus button-down collar and crocodile zip boots.

Beehives for Doowhoppers: the Ronettes in a formal pose.

Christmas with the Kennedys, with the first lady radiating the chic sophistication that took Paris by storm during the 1961 presidential visit.

Another Christian Dior cocktail/evening look for 1962. There is a touch of the "suspense-jupe" in the cut of the skirt, which is gathered tightly at the waist.

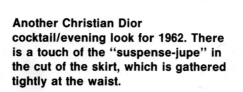

31

Beatnik Generation

Left Bank Paris

Under their calm and conservative surface, the fifties had been a period of enormous change for artists and designers in every field. By the end of the decade, some of this energy was beginning to show itself in the changing moods of jazz, cinema – and fashion.

In Paris's Saint Germaine quarter, the Left Bank movement had emerged as long ago as the forties, led by a group of writers and artists with radical new ideas that they tried to "live" on a daily basis, challenging established values and conventions. Philosopher Jean Paul Sartre and feminist Simone de Beauvoir were at the centre of this circle, which attracted a wider group

of "bohemians", including film directors François Truffaut and Roger Vadim, and jazz singer Juliette Greco.

Juliette Greco was a Left Bank fashion symbol, whether dressed in slacks and black beret or her black Balmain evening dress. The bohemians of Saint Germain gathered together to see Greco and visiting American jazz stars at notorious nightclubs such as

Le Tabou and Le Rose Rouge – notorious, that is, to non-bohemians. Another Left Bank style model was Brigitte Bardot, dressed in a tight-fitting black-and-white t-shirt or pouting from behind a tangle of curls.

Donald Byrd. 1959's *Byrd in Hand* **jacket shows the trumpeter in casual turtleneck.**

Juliette Greco, Paris Left-Bank jazz heroine.

By 1961 Byrd had gone upmarket with a Jaguar and sharp suit. But the pose remains beatnik-cool.

Allen Ginsberg at a poetry reading in 1965.

San Francisco, Heart of the Beats

Far away in California, something similar had been going on, taking its cue from young and experimental writers such as Jack Kerouac and Allen Ginsberg. Their style of writing was fast and spontaneous. Kerouac described his books *On The Road* (1957) and *The Subterraneans* (1958) as having been "written on the run", while beat poet Ginsberg believed in live performances to "capture an audience".

Beatniks were "hip", "cool" and "groovy", and considered themselves in rebellion against the "square" world of the establishment. "Hip" could be anything from be-bop jazz to Buddhism to walking in a certain way – "a catlike walk from the hips". Hip also meant turning away from the dress and even speech of the white middle class toward the music and culture of black America.

The beat style included black berets, black slacks and dark glasses. Flat shoes for the women and sandals for the men were the popular footwear. Beatnik girls were recognizable by their all-black outfits and lavish use of elaborate eye makeup. Black skirts, dancers' black leotard tops and black tights were *the* beat girl's fashion choice. Wearing the clothes might be as close as some would get to the beatnik way of life. Paris and San Francisco remained the twin centres of the beatnik universe, but groups of beatniks or beatnik imitators sprang up in towns across the world.

Playing it Cool

The beatnik message could be summed up as: "Be Cool". "Being cool" meant a completely new approach to fashion and the "right" thing to wear wasn't something from an expensive fashion house. "Being cool" meant being in the know – a very attractive idea for those with limited money to spend. The beatniks' biggest impact on fashion was in this new way of thinking about clothes. As the sixties unfolded, some beatnik attitudes worked their way into the heart of the fashion industry, through the boutique and flower-power or psychedelic revolutions. These later styles of dress – which were more startling – were to make the once-outrageous beatniks seem almost respectable.

Electric beatnik – Bob Dylan (left and right) in 1965.

Brigitte Bardot: the Paris Left Bank personified.

A more refined beatnik look for the Uptown Girl.

The Chet Baker look for "cool cats".

The Beatles: Pop Goes Fashion

Mersey Sound

The Beatles – John, Paul, George and Ringo, also known as the "Fab Four" – were four young men from Liverpool, which, like all port cities had its fair share of visitors, including American seamen, who brought the latest soul and R&B records from the US. These influences combined with a distinctive "Mersey" sound to produce a pop sensation that swept across the world in 1963 and lasted for the rest of the decade. At one point the Beatles held the top four positions in the US singles charts. This was the beginning of the "British Invasion," as groups such as the Rolling Stones, the Kinks, Manfred Mann, Herman's Hermits and The Who quickly followed up the Beatles' breakthrough. Successful though these bands were, they couldn't approach the popularity of the Beatles, whose concerts could barely be heard above the screams and cries of hysterical girls.

Pop Goes Fashion: Fashion Goes Pop

The Beatles took the trouble to keep themselves in the forefront of men's fashion. As with their music, they knew how to move on, changing their style and appeal with each successive record release. Initially, they had dressed like sixties young and hip guys in narrow black trousers, narrow-lapeled jackets, with cropped hair. But by the time of their break-

through in 1963, they had adopted the distinctive collarless Cardin suits and collar-length hair that served to make them so instantly recognizable. Long hair for men quickly became a universal sign of rebellious youth. As the sixties progressed, the Beatles moved on to "mod" styles and psychedelic outfits (see the jacket of the *Sergeant Pepper* album), finishing the decade in the casual hippie look seen on the jacket of 1969's *Abbey Road*.

The Beatles also began to attract attention from "serious" music critics. Other musicians who began to receive similar attention included Bob Dylan, Joan Baez and the Rolling Stones. This narrowing gap between classical ("serious") music and pop was mirrored by some of the changes hitting the world of fashion. Artists such as Peter Blake, Richard Hamilton and Andy Warhol began to design record jackets. Paris designers began to concentrate on their less costly ready-to-wear collections. And images from modern art began to appear on everything from dresses to grocery packaging. Fashion became caught up in an exciting revolution affecting all the arts.

George Harrison and John Lennon in 1964, at the height of Beatlemania.

**Anyone for chess? A mid-sixties
Op-Art hat and hood.**

Pop, Op and Beyond

The Pop Art movement had begun in the fifties, spearheaded by such artists as Peter Blake, Robert Rauschenberg and Andy Warhol. The key was the use of mass-produced, commercial images, often repeating them or enlarging them to concentrate attention on their deeper meaning. Pop Art has become part and parcel of fashion, and its influence continues on everything from t-shirts to Fiorucci dresses.

Op Art was a separate movement. Painters such as Victor Vasarely and Bridget Riley set out to explore and exploit the dramatic, trick-optic effects of line and contrasting areas of color. Designers such as Courrèges and Ungaro produced garments heavily influenced by Op Art, while many chain stores cashed in on the bold black-and-white theme with boots, coats and hats in contrasting PVC and other artificial fabrics. Bridget Riley's Op Art paintings were used as a basis for a series of textile designs by Julian Tomchin.

The public cheerfully mixed up Op and Pop – to the considerable annoyance of those who had started the movements. Both became just one more set of ideas to be used in the "anything goes" atmosphere of the mid-sixties.

This suit by Paris designer Courrèges is heavily influenced by Op Art in its dramatic use of black-and-white check.

One of Helmut Newton's Pop Art/Op Art fashion shots for *Queen* magazine, Spring 1966. A new generation of fashion photographers were reshaping the ways in which fashions were presented to the public.

The Monkees – a group put together specially for their own TV series, as the American answer to the Beatles. Here they are shown wearing their "uniform" of double-breasted wine-red shirts, grey slacks and wide black leather belts.

The Cardin-designed Beatle-suit, with its single-breasted collarless jacket and flapless pockets, cut lean and short and without turnups. Zip ankle boots and outrageous long hair (for 1963) complete the electrifying effect.

Peter Blake devised this cover for the Beatles' *Sergeant Pepper* album. The collage of famous faces behind the Fab Four includes Bob Dylan, Marilyn Monroe, Charlie Chaplin and Karl Marx. Waxworks of the Beatles in their earlier "mod" guise contrast with their psychedelic look (1967).

Motown, Mods and Minis

Motown Calling

The early sixties saw the Western world enjoying the benefits of the postwar industrial boom. Teenagers had few problems finding well-paid work. The teenage revolution had been a subject of conversation in the fifties, but now it gathered pace. Young people had become big spenders and a force to be reckoned with in the fashion business.

In Detroit, Smokey Robinson was spearheading the Motown record company and the new Detroit sound in soul music. Motown artists were slicker in both music and fashion than the rhythm-and-blues background from which they emerged. Smokey Robinson and the Miracles, Marvin Gaye, the Supremes, Martha and the Vandellas – all the top Motown acts had an individual style sense to go with their fresh musical approach.

Motown became known as "the home of the hits." It stood for a sophisticated black style, turning its back on the more rough-and-ready image of the city blues performers like Howling Wolf or Muddy Waters.

March of the Mods

The Motown sound caught on fast in Britain, where the Beatles were its most famous fans. And a new group of teenagers emerged in Britain with a style all their own – the mods. The mods – short for "moderns" – took their inspiration from the beatniks and also studied American college fashion for fresh ideas. The results were brightly coloured shirts and ties and turtlenecks, or, for a more relaxed look, boxy blazers and narrow pants. Mods also favoured mohair suits (as worn by the Motown artists) and liked to cover these with a green "parka" or anorak when out on their Vespa or Lambretta motor-scooters, which they rode around in packs. The Beatles looked a little like mods, but they always denied any connection with the mod movement. They wanted to appeal to everyone.

By the mid-sixties, the youth culture was having its heyday. Fashion was being made by the young for the young. Small high-fashion shops known as boutiques popped up all over North America and Europe, constantly filled with fresh ideas and new

Chart-topping all-girl group the Supremes in 1969.

Mod stars Aretha Franklin and The Who.

styles. The sales assistants were often teenagers as well, helping their contemporaries to put together a new look.

Mary Quant was one designer who understood these trends. She and her husband, Alexander Plunkett-Greene, had been building up their design and boutique empire since the late fifties, despite having no formal training in business. Quant thrived in the "do-it-yourself" atmosphere of the time. Her clothes were highly original but very inexpensive. Although her fabrics weren't always the most practical and the stitching not always the best, young girls could afford to buy one of her outfits almost every week, and the next week they could move on to something new.

Betsey Johnson's designs were making a similar impact in the US. Wilder than Quant in some ways, her mid-sixties innovations included clinging t-shirt dresses, silvery motorcycle suits, and a "noise" dress made of jersey with loose grommets attached to the hem, for built-in sound effects.

The Mini Makes It Big

Mary Quant played a key role in launching the mini-skirt. As a fashion, the mini was worn most effectively by the very young. Teamed up with geometric black-and-white Op Art patterns, the mini became an essential part of the developing mod-girl image – and the popularity of the mini-skirt spread this look all around the world. Some were shocked by skirts cut eight or nine inches above the knee – others saw the mini as a sign of greater freedom and relaxation in dress.

Models such as Twiggy, Jean Shrimpton and Penelope Tree became personifications of the mod-girl look. Wafer-thin, hair hanging loosely or cropped short in the new Vidal Sassoon cuts, their youthful or even boyish features were very different from many older models, but they fitted in perfectly with the new mood in fashion. Young girls tried to copy the "Twiggy look" of heavily made-up, "giant" eyes, and the "Shrimp look" of Jean Shrimpton, with her "bangs" of hair. Mary Quant used "Twiggy" mannequins in her chain of boutiques. Everywhere, old ideas about fashion were being turned upside-down. Youth seemed to be taking over completely, and the phrase "youth-quake" was widely used.

While Carnaby Street became the best-known fashion centre of "Swinging London", a more studied look flourished farther west in the Kings Road, Chelsea. Here an interesting mixture of English and American "college boy" dressing was seen with a hint of the approaching psychedelic explosion.

Carnaby Street, 1966: Lord John's.

The Quant look: note the variety of fabrics and colours hung on the rack, as well as the poster of Mary Quant herself in the foreground.

Off-the-rack. The simple, almost childish miniskirt became the uniform for young women, sold in boutiques and chainstores from Athens to Alaska.

The military look – not so different from the *Sergeant Pepper* jacket on page 39.

Space Age

Space Race

Space and space travel had an enormous impact on people's thinking throughout the sixties. Russia and America were engaged in a "race" to land the first man on the moon. Unmanned space missions to Venus and Mars were expanding the exploration of the solar system.

By the end of the decade (July 20, 1969) the American Apollo 11 mission had landed men on the moon – a conclusive end to that lap of the space race. In the meantime, space travel had become a major source of inspiration for both the fashion and entertainment industries.

Space Style

Barbarella (1967), starring Jane Fonda, was perhaps the most fashion-conscious space fantasy. Based on a futuristic comic strip, the movie featured bizarre and minimalist outfits in plastic and PVC – particularly for the women. See-through garments, high boots and bodysuits (or catsuits), with or without leggings, featured heavily in the film's costumes. The overall look – usually in a rather watered-down form – remained high fashion for several years after the release of the movie.

The most exclusive suit of all? Buzz Aldrin in action during the historic first moonwalk, July 20 1969. Neil Armstrong and the lunar module can be seen reflected in Aldrin's face mask.

TV's "Star Trek" and Stanley Kubrick's film *2001* took a more sober view of the future, a mood that was reflected by the wardrobe department. In fact, the outfits worn by the crews of the *Enterprise* ("Star Trek") and the *Discovery* (*2001*) were based on sketches and ideas supplied by NASA scientists. But this didn't stop fans writing in to ask where they could buy copies of the outfits for themselves.

Space-age Heroes

The space-age fever caught on at ground level, too, with heroes such as Batman and James Bond fitting the hi-tech mood very nicely. Batman and Robin drove their futuristic Batmobile and dressed in fashionable bodysuits as well – arch villain the Catwoman (Eartha Kitt) also sported a catsuit – which was only natural. Items such as

James Bond: *You Only Live Twice*.

Batman's cape and utility belt also seemed closer to being fashion accessories than serious crime-fighting equipment.

Classic James Bond films of the sixties included *Dr No*, *Goldfinger* and *You Only Live Twice*, all starring Sean Connery and all placing a strong emphasis on gadgetry, style and humour. *Goldfinger*, for example, opens with two minutes of organized mayhem, from which James Bond emerges unscathed, with a clean tuxedo beneath his rubber wetsuit. Bond's stylish adoption of traditional men's garments – dinner jacket, tuxedo, bow tie – created an image for the slightly older man that was both modern and dashing and yet suitable for formal occasions.

Space-age *Haute Couture*

However, it was in Europe rather than America that the space race made the biggest high-fashion impact. Paco Rabanne, a Spanish-trained architect turned fashion designer, created startling new styles that were widely seen as being "space age" in their approach. Instead of using traditional fabrics, Rabanne began to use discs cut from metal or plastic, linked together by wire. Metallic or dayglo colours were another key element in his collections.

The French designer Pierre Cardin was one of several others to go the space-age route in 1967. Cardin's new styles were altogether more comfortable and wearable than Rabanne's, even if his catsuits with helmets and visors did look like something straight out of the twenty-first century.

Other designers picked up on the transparent side of the space-age look, made possible by new synthetic fabrics. Rudi Gernreich, originally famed as a swimwear designer, produced collections of see-through blouses and dresses in 1968, while Courrèges showed plastic dresses with punched holes and Yves Saint Laurent a see-through blouse under a maxi-length coat in the same year. The fashion space race seemed to be about pushing back the boundaries of what was considered acceptable to wear on the street.

One of Paris designer Paco Rabanne's space-age leather outfits from 1966.

The *X-Men* – one of Marvel Comics' most popular titles in the sixties. Superheroes had been wearing space-age bodysuits since Superman burst on the scene in 1938.

How they did it in the movies (2). Barbarella's (as portrayed by Jane Fonda) "spacesuit" seems a lot less awkward to wear than astronaut Buzz Aldrin's. But unlike Aldrin, she's carrying a "gun." Note also the Buddhist "yin and yang" symbol on Barbarella's belt.

Star Trek. Chekov, Bones, Kirk and Scotty beam down to an alien planet where "no man has gone before."

Space fashions, bobby socks and wigs from Courrèges.

The Ethnic Look

Go East

By the later years of the sixties, many young people in the West had begun to take a serious interest in what was happening in the Third World. During the decade, China was going through its Cultural Revolution, and many French and British colonies had gained their independence. The "winds of change" were blowing everywhere. The Vietnam War received worldwide media coverage, and it was seen by many young people as senseless killing. There were mass demonstrations against the American government — both within the US and elsewhere.

Many young people were so impressed by the culture of the East that they began to adopt its religions, like Buddhism or the Hare Krishna sect — antimaterialist philosophies that were both personified by monks draped in linen. With travel becoming increasingly inexpensive, many young people took time out of study for the first time to discover places such as India, Afghanistan or Indonesia at first hand — on the "hippie trail" to the East.

New and old Roots

Young blacks were caught up in this mood and began to develop a stronger identity for themselves, with the help of black leaders Martin Luther King Jr., Malcolm X and Huey P. Newton. The political leadership of these men helped blacks attain a better social stance in a predominantly white society, taking more pride in their African heritage.

Fashionable clothing reflected all these movements, and many designs appeared with a heavy ethnic influence. Afghans led to kaftans. American blacks favored the unisex "dashiki" — based on the loose-fitting, vividly coloured and printed African stylings. Transparent silks in bold prints were draped freely around the body, flaunting their contrast to traditional Western ideas of cut and shape.

Beaded accessories could even be purchased in elegant stores. Fringe and tassel dresses, worn with a headband and reminiscent of native American dress, were shown at fashion shows and sold in exclusive stores. Young girls and boys carried brightly coloured woven bags imported from places such as Morocco and Turkey. Flat leather sandals — also imported — were worn by both sexes. Ethnic fashion was fanciful and unselfconscious, leaving plenty of room for individual interpretation — and not bothering too much which part of the world each piece of exotica might have come from.

Fashion for Pharaohs

Courrèges suggested an ethnic look that took ideas from the ancient Egyptians, in outfits made from heavily sequined bands, held together by transparent silk — in a look thought to resemble the wrappings of mummified pharaohs. To finish off the look, Courrèges gave his models squared-off bob wigs in metallic colours.

Young blacks in America developed their own style of revolutionary fashion. The phrase "black is beautiful" was first coined in 1968. Most young blacks stopped using chemicals to straighten their natural curls. The result was the "afro" hairstyle, traditional African hair grown to the maximum length and shaped evenly. This look was to catch on far and wide, with white contemporaries frizzing their locks in imitation. Even young Japanese were sent racing to the hairdressers to acquire an afro. Some even wore afro wigs in bright colours to join in the new exotic image. Black pop and soul stars had been leaders in the trend, and some, such as Sylvester Stewart — "Sly" of Sly and the Family Stone — sported the most spectacular hairstyles of all.

Olympic Protest

Other young blacks were influenced by the black berets and military-style clothing of the Black Panthers. Che Guevara, the Argentine-born Cuban revolutionary hero, became a model for many radical students. The Black Panthers' black beret had its "gala performance" at the 1968 Olympics in Mexico, when several medal-winning black American athletes refused to salute the Stars and Stripes during their national anthem — giving, instead, the clenched-fist salute before they stepped down from the podium.

The Black Panther uniforms of Bobby Seale (left) and Huey Newton were widely imitated, most especially among blacks.

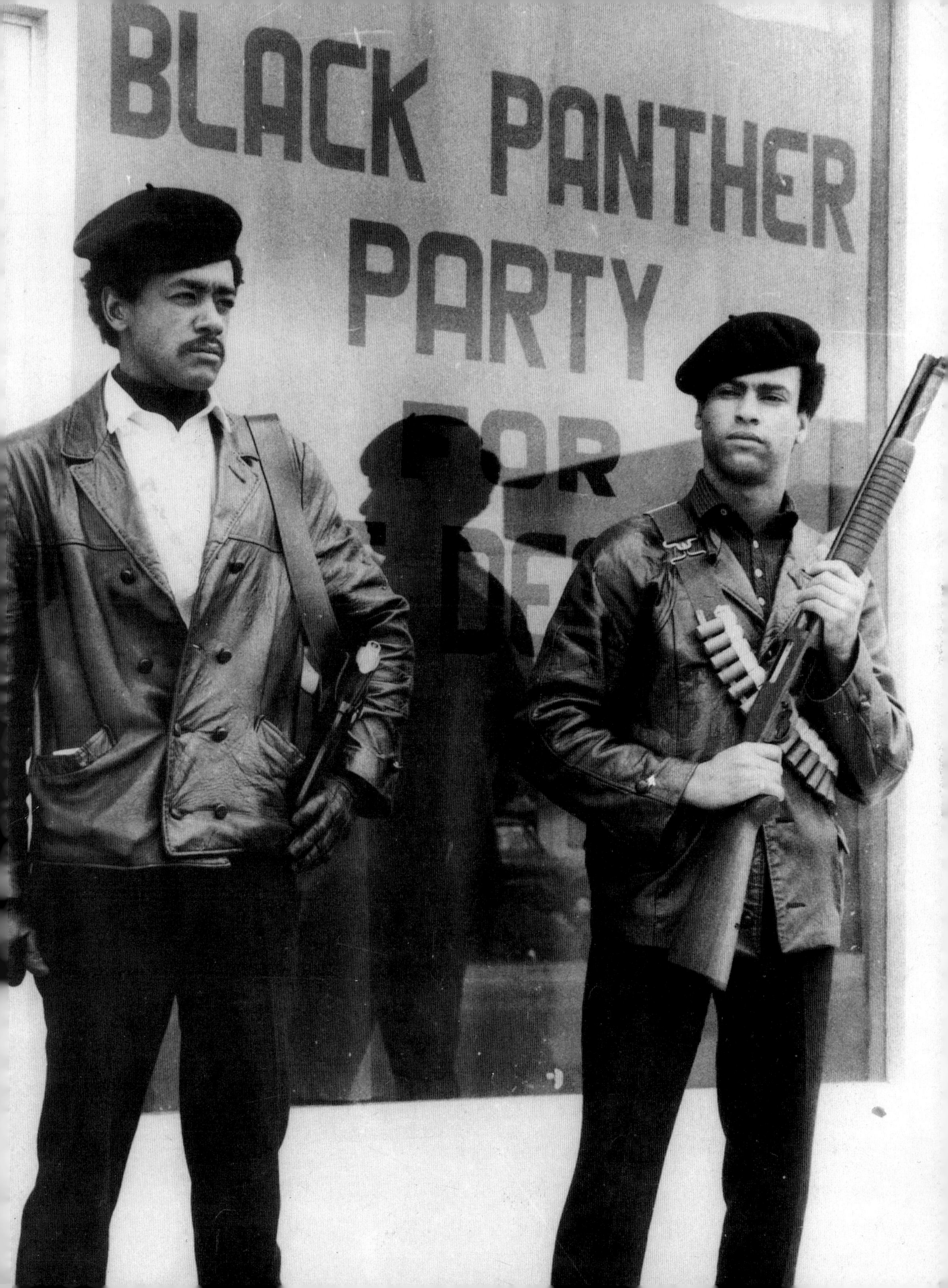
BLACK PANTHER
PARTY

As early as 1964 the fashion
magazines were featuring such
complex ethnic concoctions as this
African/Middle Eastern ensemble – a
head-scarf of North African influence
combined with vest and harem pants
of Turkish origin, a belt and bangle
that owe something to northern
India, and a very European pair of
high-heeled sandals. The setting
might be the Caribbean!

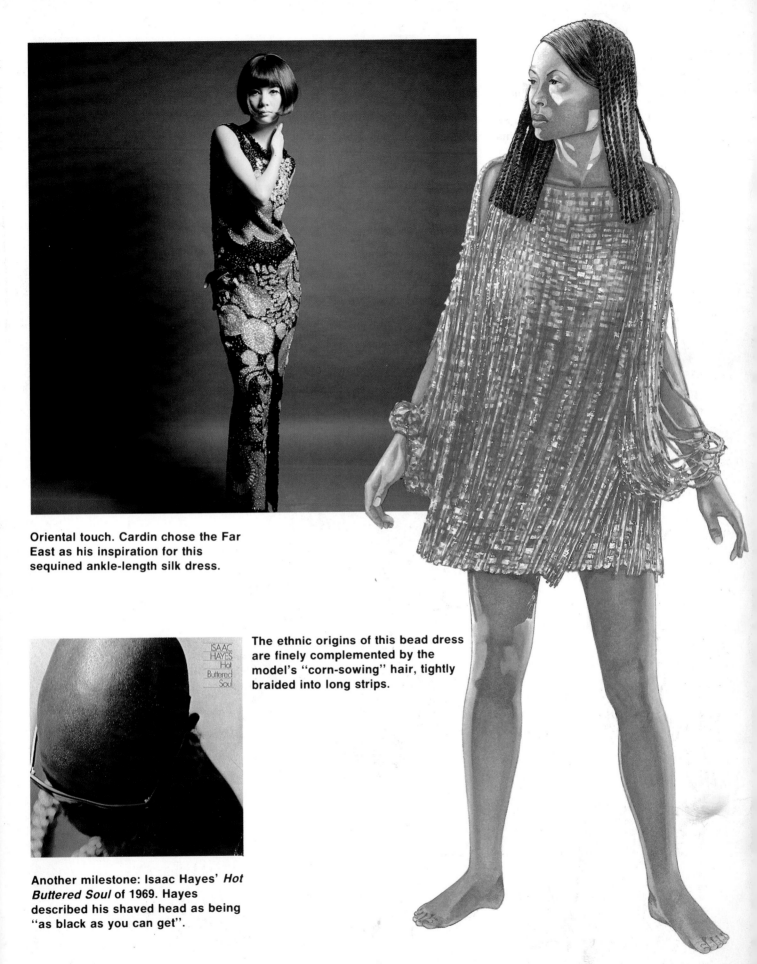

Oriental touch. Cardin chose the Far East as his inspiration for this sequined ankle-length silk dress.

The ethnic origins of this bead dress are finely complemented by the model's "corn-sowing" hair, tightly braided into long strips.

ISAAC
HAYES
Hot
Buttered
Soul

Another milestone: Isaac Hayes' *Hot Buttered Soul* of 1969. Hayes described his shaved head as being "as black as you can get".

Psychedelic Explosion

The "Underground"

Pop music was the main force behind the psychedelic explosion in the late sixties. The explosion took the form of a burst of activity in music, fashion, art, and other happenings and events never seen before.

Many of the ideas behind this movement had first surfaced in San Francisco, but the mood of the times was international, and ideas seemed to sweep along an invisible grapevine – the "underground". Underground magazines, groups and festivals sprang up all over America and Europe between 1966 and 1967.

Several young talents reached the pinnacle of their careers and then died – Janis Joplin, Otis Redding, Jimi Hendrix and Brian Jones. For the first time, soft drugs such as marijuana and hallucinogens like LSD were used outside a small circle of artists and musicians. Bob Dylan's *Blonde on Blonde* is a key record of the period. It was a time of boundless experimentation in the arts, lifestyles – and fashions.

Bold as Love

Psychedelic music took its inspiration from everywhere – the Blues, jazz, rock, electronic music, Indian music and even the classical tradition. One of the most famous musicians of the era was the guitarist and singer Jimi Hendrix.

Hendrix had begun his career as a backup musician for rhythm and blues singers like Little Richard. Stardom arrived after he moved to London in 1966 – capturing the hearts and minds of London's "in" underground club circuit. Later, he returned to the US, where he caused a sensation at the Monterey Pop Festival with his on-stage guitar-burning routine.

Also a trend-setter in his dress, Hendrix's colourful and exotic shirts, waistcoats, boots and wide-brimmed hats were frequently photographed by fashion magazines. Hendrix's elaborate jewelry was another feature of his style. But many saw him as a "wild man" and a dangerous Pied Piper, whose appearance alone was enough to start teenagers on a rampage of drugs, long hair and loud music. Hendrix was to die in mysterious circumstances in 1970.

Janis Joplin was the female personification of the psychedelic period in rock music. She had her own brand of raw energy, with a strong, gutsy voice influenced by early blues singers. As outrageous as Jimi Hendrix in her

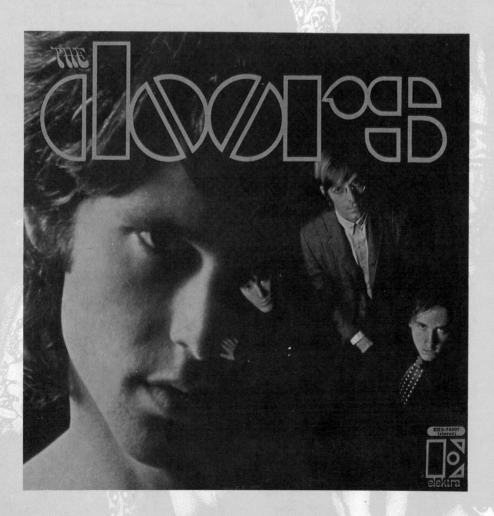

The first album by the Doors in late 1966 set the tone for a new era of highly experimental and often drug-influenced music. But it is the style of the album-jacket photography rather than the Doors' clothes which proclaim the product as "psychedelic".

lifestyle, she seemed to be on the verge of international stardom at the time of her death in 1970.

Graphic artists like Peter Max also acquired a taste for psychedelia. There was a broad turning away from self-conscious minimalism and Op Art towards fantasies using vivid "acid" colours and cartoon imagery. Posters and, above all, album covers, reflected this trend.

Sergeant Pepper

Male dress was becoming increasingly fancy and feminine – flouncy shirts in fluorescent colours, brightly printed neck scarves and beaded belts. The Beatles' costumes for the *Sergeant Pepper* album jacket (1967) are a classic example of psychedelic dress for men – brightly coloured old-style military uniforms, in which the band posed like flower-power Napoleons. In making even these kinds of clothes into a psychedelic statement, the Beatles undercut a stronghold of masculine conformity. Released at the height of the Vietnam War, the significance of these freaked-out uniforms would not have been lost on fans.

Fashion designers responded to the psychedelic mood by strengthening their colours. Bright and bold, purple and orange flower prints on velvet fabrics were made into tight-fitting trousers for men. The trend was completely international. The Italian designer Emilio Pucci gave his clothes both a richness of colour, and brilliant patterns. He made use of newly-devised stretch fabrics in his tightly-fitting dresses and trousers.

Fiorucci developed an equally youthful approach to fashion, using pop styles to create his own particular brand of chic. Bright colours and animal prints on dresses and skirts remained his hallmark even in the eighties. Psychedelia lives on.

The late Jimi Hendrix, singer, guitarist and psychedelic standard-bearer, in 1967.

Oz, 1968. One of the most famous of the underground magazines of the late sixties, *Oz* featured psychedelic graphics coupled with the early writings of Germaine Greer, Clive James and others.

Janis Joplin, Woodstock Festival, 1969.

The sharp, brilliantly glowing "acid" blues, greens and purples became a trademark of Emilio Pucci, Italy's noted designer. Here a tunic top is worn over slim leggings and coordinated ankle boots.

Cream's *Disraeli Gears*, 1968. Just how psychedelic can you get?

Fabric designed by Emilio Pucci in the late sixties. The design is similar (but not identical) to the pants suit illustrated on page 54.

Striped pants, waistcoat, t-shirt, "granny" glasses, love-beads, droopy moustache and long hair – almost a uniform for musicians and their hangers-on in the late sixties.

Helmut Newton's version of Paris psychedelia for *Vogue*, 1966.

Flower Power Goes High Fashion

The Hippie Dream

The original hippies living in San Francisco in the mid-sixties could never have imagined that their crazy style of dressing would have been transformed into high fashion by the end of the decade. Theirs was an "anti-style," which rejected the "work ethic" of Western society, along with the conformist clothing it encouraged. Hippies had shocked and intrigued with their communal life-styles, belief in free love, and experiments with drugs. Tourists flocked to the Haight-Ashbury neighbourhood of San Francisco to see these strange beings in sandals and kaftans, handing out flowers as symbols of peace and love. Others talked of an "alternative society" and of establishing self-supporting rural communities of like-minded people.

In complete contrast to the clean, geometric lines of the "space-age" look, hippies decorated everything, even painting their bodies. Psychedelic, ethnic and a romanticized view of the past all jostled together. The hippie woman would not wear a teasing miniskirt, but a floor-length one accessorized with love-beads and bells. The hippie man, with flowing robe and long loose hair, presented much the same outline – challenging society's ideas about masculinity. "You can't tell the boys from the girls" was the outraged response.

Hair and Hemlines

But it wasn't necessary to be a full-time hippie. By 1967, the "Summer of Love," the fashionable young of America and Europe had taken up the hippie look – though not always the hippie way of life. In an era of increasing affluence, they could afford to show contempt for money and work. *Hair*, the "tribal love-rock musical," went to Broadway in April 1968, and then to London – and was a smash hit everywhere.

Everyone started to grow their hair long – by 1969, even well-groomed Twiggy wanted hers to her waist. Long hair for boys was often discouraged or banned in schools, while the long maxiskirt – a hippie spinoff – aroused the same anger as the mini. Many girls flaunted both fashions, wearing the shortest of skirts under the longest of coats.

The Beatles continued to grow their hair still longer, and they adopted not only hippie fashions but many of the hippie ideas. In January 1968 they set up Apple Corps Ltd, an attempt to organize business on terms of complete trust. The Apple boutique in London opened with great fanfare, and the fashions were featured in *Vogue*, but it closed before the end of the year, with huge losses.

Miners – a mass-market cosmetics company – was quick to cash in on the wide-eyed hippie look of 1966–67.

Money changing hands at the Apple boutique, early 1969.

The Designer Hippie

Paris designers flung themselves into the new mood with enthusiasm. The hippies' cheap, flamboyant clothes were transformed into expensive designer wear and became embraced by the establishment. The ready-to-wear collections of January 1967 were full of Oriental touches, striped *djella-bas*, harem dresses, tent dresses, rajah coats, Nehru jackets, in fine wools and exotic silks.

For men, jewelry collections were launched to wear over loose billowing shirts, and velvet trousers with wide bottoms. The look was soft and feminine. For women, Yves Saint Laurent produced long highwayman coats. Everyone could dress up in the style of another country, another age, another sex. Antifashion had become the biggest fashion of all.

By 1969 there seemed to be no hard and fast rules any more. Some designers, notably Courrèges, continued with the short, sharp mini, and the "space age" look was given a new lease of life when Apollo 11 landed men on the moon. But most began to follow the hippie ideal of "doing your own thing." "The length of your skirt is how you feel this moment" reported *Vogue*. The designers agreed, and the final collections of the sixties embraced the microskirt and the maxi, along with the compromise midi. Antifashion had triumphed in a roundabout way, and nothing would ever be quite the same again.

Twiggy – transformed from a Swinging Sixties mod girl to a brooding, high-fashion hippie, in this "ethnic" costume of 1969.

Fruit power! New York's Velvet Underground gained pop culture's ultimate seal of approval with this album cover by artist and style guru Andy Warhol.

Flowers everywhere in this kaftan designed by Vancetti for spring 1969 – topped by an African-influenced hairstyle.

Hot Rats! The shock value of the underground culture was harnessed to promote Frank Zappa's experimental, jazz-influenced music – even though Zappa himself opposed almost all the ideals of the hippie culture.

The Beatles and their cardboard cutouts in a publicity shot for the movie *Yellow Submarine*, which cunningly packaged the psychedelic mood for a mass public. The Beatles began their "flower power" phase in designer outfits, but seemed bored by it all by 1969, when they began to dress more like the average hippie next door.

If you couldn't afford a Bentley like John Lennon, it was okay to repaint your mini or VW Beetle.

By 1968, fashion leaders such as photographer Patrick Lichfield were combining Flower Power ideas with a "Regency Dandy" image. Dressed like this, aristocrats and pop stars could compete on equal terms for attention.

Glossary

Afro Naturally grown, long, bushy hairstyle widely adopted by blacks in America in the 1960s. Created by artificial methods, the style also became popular among whites during the late sixties and early seventies.

Apple Corps Ltd An organization set up by the Beatles in 1968 to control their own record label as well as other business and artistic ventures, including two Apple boutiques in London. Apple Corps and the boutiques folded after less than one year, though the record label survived.

Barbarella Film directed by Roger Vadim, released in 1967. The movie stars Jane Fonda as an interplanetary adventurer and features fantastic and innovative space-age costumes designed by Jaques Fonteray.

Bates, John (b. 1935) British designer. Worked as a fashion illustrator in the fifties before forming the Varnon company in 1964, where he produced exciting range of youthful designs, including pantsuits, catsuits and string-vest dresses. Bates also designed the costumes for the Emma Peel character in the TV series "The Avengers".

Beene, Geoffrey (b. 1927) US designer. Worked in Paris in the forties, and later in New York. In 1963 he set up his own company, gaining a reputation for his simple, youthful shifts and t-shirt dresses. Beene's other influential work in the late sixties included designs with sequinned fabrics, chiffon, jersey and taffeta.

Cardin, Pierre (b. 1927) French designer. Worked with Paquin, Schiaparelli and Dior before producing his first collection in 1957. His career blossomed in the sixties, with cut-out dresses, space-age catsuits, tight leather pants, bodystockings and other concepts that became inseparable from "space-age" sixties fashion.

Cashin, Bonnie (b. 1915) US designer, born in Oakland, California. Worked in costume design for Hollywood, before opening her own fashion business in New York in 1949. A great mixer of fabrics, especially leather, canvas and suede, and a clever adapter of ethnic influences, Cashin's work was an important influence on the direction of sixties fashion, and many of the fashions of more recent years.

Chanel, Coco (1883–1971) French designer, designing under her own label since 1914. Extremely influential and innovative in the twenties and thirties and later through her introduction of the "Chanel suit." By the sixties, the Chanel suit had re-emerged to gain the classic status it still enjoys today.

Clark, Ossie (b. 1942) British designer, working for the Quorum boutique from the early sixties. Clark was an influential figure on the Kings Road fashion scene throughout the decade, producing gypsy dresses, motorcycle jackets and innovative work in leather and snakeskin.

Courrèges, André (b. 1923) French designer. He worked for Balenciaga before opening his own house in 1961. A leading figure in the introduction of the miniskirt and pantsuit, Courrèges also became known as a space-age designer for his catsuits, see-through dresses and futuristic goggles and boots. A key figure in the fashions of the sixties.

Dior, Christian (1905–57) French designer, who revolutionized postwar fashion with his New Look of 1947. After Dior's death, the House of Dior was led by French designer Marc Bohan (b. 1926), who successfully carried Dior's reputation for elegance into the decade of pop fashions.

Djellabah Hooded cloak, Moroccan in origin, with long, wide sleeves, worn open at the neck and reaching as far as the knee.

Dorothée Bis Chain of stores opened by Elie and Jaqueline Jacobson in Paris and later in the USA. From 1962 the chain specialized in adult versions of young girls' clothes – knee socks, peaked caps and ribbed knitwear.

Fiorucci, Elio (b. 1935) Italian designer and entrepreneur, born in Milan. Fiorucci inherited a shoe store from his father, and soon expanded the shop's stock to include miniskirts. In 1967 he opened a larger store, and from this base built up his world-famous chain of boutiques conceived with the young consumer in mind.

Fogarty, Anne (1919–1981) US designer, who worked for many clients, including Saks Fifth Avenue, for whom she designed from 1957. A significant influence in the fifties, Fogarty responded creatively to the challenge of the sixties with culottes, miniskirts and other simple, wearable designs.

Gernreich, Rudi (1922–85) Austrian-born designer, working in the USA from 1938, and designing under his own name from 1951. In 1964 he formed Rudi Gernreich Inc. Gernreich was an influential designer of sportswear, separates and shirtwaists, as well as the swimwear and underwear he is best remembered for today – including bodystockings and radically engineered bras for low-neck and plunge-back evening wear.

Givenchy, Hubert (b. 1927) French designer who worked for Schiaparelli before opening his own business in 1952. An important influence on the elegant cocktail and evening dress look of the late fifties and early sixties, Givenchy's designs were a favourite with (amongst others) First Lady Jackie Kennedy.

Johnson, Betsey (b. 1942) American designer, born in Hartford, Connecticut. On graduating from Syracuse University in 1964, she became an editor at *Madamoiselle* magazine, while designing clothes in her spare time. In 1965 she was widely hailed as a radical and exciting new designer. Johnson continued to innovate through the sixties, with pantsuits, miniskirts, t-shirt dresses, and many other novelties. In 1969 she opened her own New York boutique called "Betsey, Bunky and Mini," and has in more recent years turned to the design of disco and sportswear.

Khanh, Emanuelle (b. 1937) French designer who worked for Dorothée Bis and Cacharel in the sixties, establishing her own label in 1970. Khanh's sixties designs included long droopy collars on jackets, dresses and blouses, frilly miniskirts, and lined outfits with lace trimming. Her name is associated with the French "Ye Ye" fashions of the sixties – designs taking their nickname from the Beatles' song "She Loves You, Yeah Yeah Yeah."

Nehru Jacket Straight, slim, hip-length jacket, buttoned in front to a straight, standing collar, based on the design of a jacket popularized by Jawarharlal Nehru, Indian prime minister 1947–64.

Op Art Art movement prominent in the 1960s, and extremely influential on fashion and textile design. Op Art exploits the dramatic "trick optic" effects of contrasting areas of colour and black-and-white.

Parka Hooded garment similar to an anorak, but usually longer and more loosely cut. Popular outerwear for mods.

Pop Art Art movement having its origins in the fifties, but very widely influential on fashion and much else in the sixties. Pop Art makes use of ready-made images from consumer society, concentrating the viewer's attention by enlarging them or offering them in a startling new context.

Pucci, Emilio (b. 1914) Italian designer. A doctor of political science and part of the Italian Olympic skiiing team, Pucci entered the world of fashion through the design of sportswear. His boldly patterned fabrics for skirts, dresses and pantsuits captured the psychedelic mood of the late sixties very effectively.

Quant, Mary (b. 1934) British designer. Opened her first shop in 1955, and founded the Ginger Group label in 1963. Quant's bright, simple and well-coordinated designs were perfectly in tune with the mood of the 1960s. Quant's innovations included the miniskirt, coloured tights, skinny-rib sweaters and a range of wet-look PVC fashions.

Rabanne, Paco (b. 1934) Spanish designer who studied architecture in Paris from 1952 to 1964. Rabanne's architectural background led to dresses made from plastic, metal discs and chains instead of conventional fabrics. Rabanne opened his own house in 1966, and continued to be a key influence on the "space age" styles of the decade.

Ready-to-Wear Clothes carrying a designer label that can be bought ready-made from the hanger.

Saint Laurent, Yves (b. 1936) French designer, who worked successfully for Christian Dior before opening his own house in 1962. Saint Laurent's inventive genius was ideally matched to the mood of the sixties and he produced a seemingly endless parade of startling but much-imitated designs: pea jackets, smocks in jersey and silk, knickerbockers, see-through blouses, pantsuits, safari suits and so on. Saint Laurent opened his own ready-to-wear chain, *Rive Gauche*, in 1966. He remains a key figure in the development of modern fashion.

Reading List

A great deal has been written and published about the nineteen sixties – this reading list is only a very small selection. Magazines and movies of the period are another excellent source of information.

Adult General Reference Sources

Calasibetta, Charlotte, *Essential Terms of Fashion: A Collection of Definitions* (Fairchild, 1985).

Calasibetta, Charlotte, *Fairchild's Dictionary of Fashion*, 2nd Edition (Fairchild, 1988).
Gold, Annalee, *90 Years of Fashion* (Fairchild, 1990).
O'Hara, Georgina, *The Encyclopedia of Fashion* (Harry N. Abrams, 1986).
Trahey, Jane (Ed.), *100 Years of the American Female From Harper's Bazaar* (Random House, 1967).

Young Adult Sources

Ruby, Jennifer, *The Nineteen Sixties & Nineteen Seventies*, "Costume in Context" series (David & Charles, 1989).
Wilcox, R. Turner, *Five Centuries of American Costume* (Scribner's, 1963).

Acknowledgments

The Author and Publishers would like to thank the following for permission to reproduce illustrations: The Camera Press for pages 7, 8, 13, 17, 22, 28, 31(b), 38(b), 43(c), 51(a), 55(d), 57, 58(d), 59(a), 63; The Hulton Picture Company for pages 12, 20, 21, 33(b) and 36; NASA for page 44; Popperfoto for page 9; David Redferns for pages 26 and 54(a); Rex Features for pages 6, 10, 14, 18, 23, 29, 30(b), 30(c), 32(b), 34(b), 37, 38(c), 43(a), 43(b), 47(a), 47(c) and 59(b). The illustrations were researched by David Pratt.

Time Chart

NEWS	**EVENTS**	**FASHIONS**
60 American U2 spy plane shot down over USSR John F. Kennedy elected US President Rome Olympics	*La Dolce Vita* (Fellini) and *Psycho* (Hitchcock) are among the new movies released	Marc Bohan becomes artistic director for Dior
61 Berlin Wall goes up Stalin's body removed from Red Square in Moscow Yuri Gagarin first man in space	Salvation plan for the Abu Simbel temple in Egypt, threatened by rising waters from the Aswan dam	Courrèges opens his own house Emanuelle Khanh achieves prominence in France, with designs featured in *Elle* magazine
62 Arrest of ANC leader Nelson Mandela in South Africa John Glenn achieves first US orbital space flight Cuba missile crisis	"Love Me Do", the first Beatles single *Dr No*, the first James Bond movie, is released	Saint Laurent opens his own business Dorothée Bis chain opens
63 Profumo scandal in Britain Alec Douglas Home becomes British Prime Minister President Kennedy assassinated: Lyndon Johnson becomes US President	Beatlemania, as the group from Liverpool top charts around the world Folk music scene at peak in US: Bob Dylan and Joan Baez are leading exponents	Cardin Beatle suits Mary Quant starts Ginger Group label Geoffrey Beene forms his own company
64 Trial of Nelson Mandela Labour Party win elections in Britain: Harold Wilson becomes Prime Minister	Beatles achieve top four positions in US singles charts "British Invasion" of bands follows in the Beatles' wake	Rudi Gernreich Inc. is formed Cardin "Space Age" collection
65 Watts riots in Los Angeles Lyndon Johnson takes Kennedy's Civil Rights Bill through Congress	*The Red Desert* (Antonioni) and *The Knack* are two of the year's most talked-about movies Bob Dylan "goes electric," infuriating many folk music fans	Mini-skirts climb far above the knee Plastic dress from Paco Rabanne Betsey Johnson makes impact as designer while working as editor for *Madamoiselle* magazine
66 France leaves NATO Cultural Revolution officially begins in China	Psychedelic movement in music and fashion begins to gather pace	Saint Laurent opens *Rive Gauche* ready-to-wear chain. His couture collection features a "smoking" jacket for women Paco Rabanne forms his own label Twiggy emerges as the decade's most famous model
67 Six Day War in the Middle East	Beatles release *Sergeant Pepper*, a psychedelic record inside a psychedelic pop art cover *Barbarella* is released, as is the gangster movie *Bonnie and Clyde*. Both are hugely successful	Fiorucci begins the expansion of his family business Psychedelic and ethnic fashions begin to appear in the designer collections
68 Tet Offensive in Vietnam: US involvement reaches its peak Assassination of Robert Kennedy and Martin Luther King Jr.	The Beatles' movie *Yellow Submarine* opens, the Beatles' Apple boutique opens and closes Black Power demonstrations by medal-winning US athletes at the Mexico Olympics *2001: A Space Odyssey* is released	Balenciaga retires Saint Laurent see-through blouse and safari jacket
69 Border clashes between USSR and China The "Troubles" begin in Northern Ireland US Apollo 11 Astronauts land on Moon	Woodstock festival: peace and love triumphant	Afro hairstyles begin to catch on with whites as well as blacks Maxi and midi lengths begin to gain ground Saint Laurent introduces pantsuits

Minis galore: space-age fashions shown at Maxim's in 1966 by (left to right) Emanuelle Khanh, Paco Rabanne, Emanuelle Khanh and Michelle Rosier.

INDEX